Copyright

Copyright © 2024 Sophie McKay

Published in the United States of America, 2024

Legal Notice: This book is copyright protected. This book is only for personal use. All rights reserved. No portion of this book may be reproduced, stored in a retrieval system, or transmitted in any form or by any means – electronic, mechanical, photocopy, recording, or any other – except for brief quotations in a book review, without the prior written permission of the author or publisher.

For more information, contact www.sophiemckay.com
First edition, 2024
ISBN 978-1-916662-12-4 (paperback)
ISBN 978-1-916662-13-1 (hardcover)

Website: www.SmartMindPublishing.com
Email: Sophie@sophiemckay.com
Author page: https://www.facebook.com/Sophie.McKay.Author
Facebook: www.facebook.com/groups/garden.to.table.tribe

How to Use This Journal

Welcome to your new guided fruit tree gardening journal and logbook! This resource is designed to assist you in nurturing your fruit trees and capturing the journey of cultivating delicious harvests at home. Whether you're a beginner or an experienced gardener, this journal is tailored to complement the insights shared in the "Beginner's Guide to Growing Fruit Trees at Home" book. Still, it's equally valuable for those who may not own the main guide, as I will give you helpful advice along the way. You may wonder how to begin, but don't worry; it's simple!

First, acquaint yourself with the various sections of this journal, such as the orchard goals, tree inventory, and seasonal planner. Then, begin documenting the specific details relevant to your fruit trees. No need to rush—savor the process of brainstorming, observing, and tracking your progress. This journal is your ally, offering guidance and organization, so relax, keep it simple, and enjoy the experience.

The beauty of keeping notes in this journal lies in the ability to revisit them next year and replicate your successes. If you encountered challenges last year, use these notes to learn and adapt for future fruit tree seasons.

Make this journal a repository for exciting moments in your orchard and a reminder of future endeavors. I've also included illustrations for you to color, adding a personal touch to your gardening diary. Let your creativity bloom as you unwind in the midst of your fruitful haven.

Wishing you the best of luck and a season of joyous fruit tree gardening!

Sophie

Table of contents

Plans for The Year	6
What do I want from my dream garden?	7
Goals Planner and Action Plan	9
Tools Inventory and Shopping List	12
My Wish List	13
My Shopping List	14
My Favorite Nurseries and Suppliers	15
Family Food Needs Tracker	18
Garden Expense Tracker	22
The no-spend challenge	24
Know Your Place! Garden Notes and Observations	25
Garden Notes and Observations	27
Garden Layout and Sun Map	29
A Moment of Joy -Picnic in My Garden	32
Shrubs and Berries Garden Bed Planner	33
Garden Planner	36
Tree Planting Log	38
My Pruning Glossary	40
Pruning Basics	41
How to Do the First Spring and Summer Pruning	43
Tree Pruning Log	45
My Calendar	48
Planting, Blooming, and Harvesting Timeline	56
Early Spring : Seasonal Chore Planner, Tasks and Review	60
Late Spring : Seasonal Chore Planner, Tasks and Review	61
Early Summer : Seasonal Chore Planner, Tasks and Review	63
Late Summer : Seasonal Chore Planner, Tasks and Review	64
Fall: Seasonal Chore Planner, Tasks and Review	66
Winter: Seasonal Chore Planner, Tasks and Review	68
Bringing Old Trees to Life	70
Tree Rejuvenating Action Plan	71
Plant Profiles	75
Composting Basics	95
Rainfall Recording Sheet and Watering Tracker	97
Water Saving Ideas for the Future	101
Pest and Disease Tracker	102
Bring the Bees to the Yard	106
Pollinator Fan Page	107
Harvest Tracking Sheet	114
Ready for some more inspiration?	117
Notes	118
Dot Grid Planner	129
Link to download free, printable pages for your log book	136

My Quick Links
(my personal table of contents)

Plans for The Year

You can use this page to brainstorm and plan what you want to achieve in your fruit tree garden this year. Write your thoughts into the speech bubbles on the following page, bringing together all the ideas and inspirations for your orchard, then summarize your final decisions below.

Remember, it's important to set simple and realistic goals, so you don't feel overwhelmed. Think about what you want from your garden. For example, do you want to grow your own food, create a relaxing outdoor space, rejuvenate and old tree, or attract pollinators?

Once you've decided on your goals, it's time to come up with a plan to reach them. Maybe you need to do some research on tree varieties, invest in some new tools, do some pruning or start a compost pile.

Remember to maintain detailed notes throughout the season, so that you can replicate successful approaches and learn from any challenges. Your fruit tree journal is your guide to a fruitful and rewarding gardening experience.

"He who plants a tree plants hope.."

Lucy Larcom
American poet and teacher

Brainstorming Page
What do I want from my dream garden?

Brainstorming Page
What do I want from my dream garden?

Final decisions

Goals Planner and Action Plan

Use this page to break down your fruit garden goals into actionable tasks. Having your goals broken down into more achievable sections will help you avoid stress and procrastination, but remember that you can always change things if needed.

MY MAIN GOAL:
....
....
....

MILESTONE / STEP 1

MILESTONE / STEP 2

MILESTONE / STEP 3

ACTIONS
- ☐ ....
- ☐ ....
- ☐ ....
- ☐ ....
- ☐ ....
- ☐ ....
- ☐ ....
- ☐ ....

ACTIONS
- ☐ ....
- ☐ ....
- ☐ ....
- ☐ ....
- ☐ ....
- ☐ ....
- ☐ ....
- ☐ ....

ACTIONS
- ☐ ....
- ☐ ....
- ☐ ....
- ☐ ....
- ☐ ....
- ☐ ....
- ☐ ....
- ☐ ....

TARGET DATE

TARGET DATE

TARGET DATE

Goals Planner and Action Plan

MY GOAL:

....
....
....
....

MILESTONE / STEP 1	MILESTONE / STEP 2	MILESTONE / STEP 3

ACTIONS	ACTIONS	ACTIONS
☐	☐	☐ ....
☐	☐	☐ ....
☐	☐	☐ ....
☐	☐	☐ ....
☐	☐	☐ ....
☐	☐	☐ ....
☐	☐	☐ ....
☐	☐	☐ ....

TARGET DATE	TARGET DATE	TARGET DATE
☐	☐	☐

Goals Planner and Action Plan

MY GOAL:

....
....
....
....

MILESTONE / STEP 1	MILESTONE / STEP 2	MILESTONE / STEP 3

ACTIONS ACTIONS ACTIONS

- ☐ ....
- ☐ ....
- ☐ ....
- ☐ ....
- ☐ ....
- ☐ ....
- ☐ ....
- ☐ ....

TARGET DATE	TARGET DATE	TARGET DATE

Tools Inventory and Shopping List

At the start of the season, check your garden tools! Mark the tools you already have and don't need to be fixed or changed. Below you can create a list of what you still need to purchase.

My Wish List

SEEDS AND PLANTS
☐
☐
☐
☐
☐
☐
☐
☐
☐

GARDEN TOOLS
☐
☐
☐
☐
☐
☐
☐
☐
☐

SUPPLIES
☐
☐
☐
☐
☐
☐
☐
☐
☐

OTHERS
☐
☐
☐
☐
☐
☐
☐
☐
☐

My Shopping List

SEEDS AND PLANTS
☐
☐
☐
☐
☐
☐
☐
☐
☐

GARDEN TOOLS
☐
☐
☐
☐
☐
☐
☐
☐
☐

SUPPLIES
☐
☐
☐
☐
☐
☐
☐
☐
☐

OTHERS
☐
☐
☐
☐
☐
☐
☐
☐
☐

My Favorite Nurseries and Suppliers

| Name: .... |
| Phone:.. |
| Email: .... |
| Address: .... |
| Notes: .... |

| Name: .... |
| Phone:.. |
| Email: .... |
| Address: .... |
| Notes: .... |

| Name: .... |
| Phone:.. |
| Email: .... |
| Address: .... |
| Notes: .... |

| Name: .... |
| Phone:.. |
| Email: .... |
| Address: .... |
| Notes: .... |

| Name: .... |
| Phone:.. |
| Email: .... |
| Address: .... |
| Notes: .... |

| Name: .... |
| Phone:.. |
| Email: .... |
| Address: .... |
| Notes: .... |

| Name: .... |
| Phone:.. |
| Email: .... |
| Address: .... |
| Notes: .... |

| Name: .... |
| Phone:.. |
| Email: .... |
| Address: .... |
| Notes:.. |

My Favorite Nurseries and Suppliers

Name: .... Phone: .... Email: .... Address: .... Notes:	Name: .... Phone: .... Email: .... Address: .... Notes: ....
Name: .... Phone: .... Email: .... Address: .... Notes:	Name: .... Phone: .... Email: .... Address: .... Notes: ....
Name: .... Phone: .... Email: .... Address: .... Notes:	Name: .... Phone: .... Email: .... Address: .... Notes: ....
Name: .... Phone: .... Email: .... Address: .... Notes:	Name: .... Phone: .... Email: .... Address: .... Notes: ....

My Favorite Nurseries and Suppliers

Name: ....
Phone: ....
Email: ....
Address: ....
Notes: ....

Name: ....
Phone: ....
Email: ....
Address: ....
Notes: ....

Name: ....
Phone: ....
Email: ....
Address: ....
Notes: ....

Name: ....
Phone: ....
Email: ....
Address: ....
Notes: ....

Name: ....
Phone: ....
Email: ....
Address: ....
Notes: ....

Name: ....
Phone: ....
Email: ....
Address: ....
Notes: ....

Name: ....
Phone: ....
Email: ....
Address: ....
Notes: ....

Name: ....
Phone: ....
Email: ....
Address: ....
Notes: ....

Family Food Needs Tracker

Welcome to your family food needs tracker! This tool is designed to assist you in planning and cultivating your own assortment of fruits at home. By gauging the quantity of fruits your family consumes each week, you can strategically decide how much of each fruit to grow. Don't forget to factor in preservation methods for an abundant harvest!

This tracker aids in designing your family's personal home orchard, ensuring you cultivate the fruits your loved ones enjoy the most. For instance, if your family consumes two pounds of apples weekly, you can estimate that a certain number of apple trees are needed to meet this requirement throughout the growing season. Consider growing extra to preserve for later use!

The specific quantity and number of trees will depend on your family's preferences, the variety of chosen apples, and the growing conditions in your area. To assist you, here's a basic table example to keep track of your family's fruit needs. Feel free to modify the numbers to tailor your garden plan to suit your family's unique preferences and requirements.

Fruits & Vegetables	Amount needed per week	Monthly amount	Avg yield of 1 plant of the chosen variety	Number of plants needed per season
Green apples for the kids	28 pieces	120 pcs	150 pounds	1 tree
Plums for pies + jam	3 pounds	12 pounds	70-90 pounds / variety	2 trees
Strawberries	2 pounds	12 pounds	1 pound / season	15-20 plants

You can also include your family's vegetable needs!

Family Food Needs Tracker

Fruits & Vegetables	Amount needed per week	Monthly amount	Avg yield of 1 plant of the chosen variety	Number of plants needed per season

Family Food Needs Tracker

Fruits & Vegetables	Amount needed per week	Monthly amount	Avg yield of 1 plant of the chosen variety	Number of plants needed per season

Family Food Needs Tracker

Fruits & Vegetables	Amount needed per week	Monthly amount	Avg yield of 1 plant of the chosen variety	Number of plants needed per season

Garden Expense Tracker

DATE	ITEM / DESCRIPTION	QTY	PLANNED COST	ACTUAL COST
			TOTAL	

NOTES

Garden Expense Tracker

DATE	ITEM / DESCRIPTION	QTY	PLANNED COST	ACTUAL COST
			TOTAL	

NOTES

The no-spend challenge

A no-spend challenge for gardeners not only encourages using what you already have but also promotes community building and sharing resources. Gardeners can exchange plants, seedlings and grafts, or even borrow tools with their neighbors, creating a community and reducing waste by avoiding unnecessary purchases.

START DATE.................................... END DATE......................................

RULES:
....
....
....
....
....
....
....
....

MY DO NOT BUY LIST

- ☐ ....
- ☐ ....
- ☐ ....
- ☐ ....
- ☐ ....
- ☐ ....
- ☐ ....

EXCEPTIONALS FROM THE RULES

Know Your Place!
Garden Notes and Observations

Observing your garden or even your patio or balcony (for container-size dwarf trees) is critical to planning and building a good growing place. You can discover the optimum sites for plants and other garden equipment by spending time in your outside space and monitoring the patterns of sunshine, shadow, and wind.

Here's a short questionnaire to help you find the best location for your trees. Carefully observe your backyard and ask yourself the following questions. Write down the answers on a sheet of paper and refer to it when choosing trees or positioning them in your backyard.

The Sun
- How many hours of sunlight does your location receive: Full sun (6+ hrs), partial sun (3-6 hrs), or full shade (<3 hours)?
- Remember that most fruit trees require six or more hours of direct light.
- Some varieties such as pawpaw, Saskatoon berry, Cornelian cherry, and hazelnut can survive in partial shade.

The Soil
- What kind of soil does your area have?
- Is it well draining?
- Does it contain healthy soil life such as earthworms?
- Does it contain an adequate level of organic matter?
- Is it rich in nutrients and minerals?

The Wind
- Does your area get a lot of strong wind?
- Does it receive chilly winds during the winter?

The Water
- How much rainfall does your location get?

Know Your Place!
All about the sun

Different areas in your yard receive different amounts of sunlight. Before you begin planting, study the amount of sun the area you've chosen for your orchard receives throughout the day. Is it covered in shade? Does it get morning or afternoon sun? Is it bright and sunny 24/7? Will any large trees or buildings in the surrounding area cast shadows on the spot you've chosen? And finally, what are the sunlight requirements of your trees?

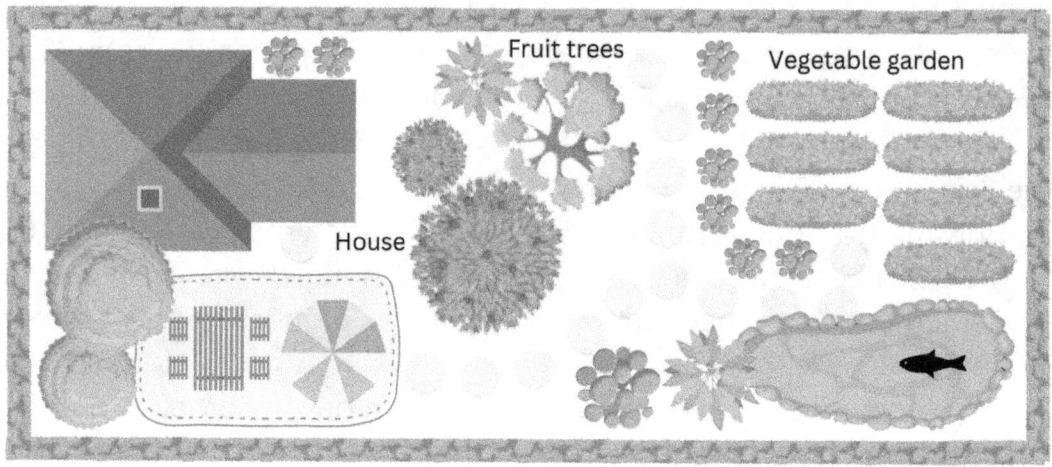

You can easily find the sun requirements of the trees you plan to grow online or check their labels at the gardening center. Fruit trees need a lot of sun while few varieties can manage in partial shade; however, a general rule of thumb to remember while setting up a home orchard is that more sun equals more fruit.

Using these designs will help you maximize your available area and create a beautiful, healthy garden, regardless of how big or tiny it is.

Zone	Time			
	9 AM	11 AM	2 PM	6 PM
West wall	Shade	Partial sun	Full sun - very hot	Full sun
Apple tree area	Partial sun	Sun	Sun	Sun
Frontyard garden	Shade	Partial sun	Partial sun	Sun
Fireplace zone	Shade	Shade	Partial sun	Sun
Near the fence	Sun	Full sun	Partial sun	Shade - often windy

Garden Notes and Observations

You can make notes about the different areas on your property. This will help you choose the best plants for each zone.

Zone	Time			

Garden Notes and Observations

You can make notes about the different areas on your property. This will help you choose the best plants for each zone.

Zone	Time			

Garden Layout and Sun Map

You can draw your backyard, garden or even your patio here. Don't worry too much about how precise your drawing is. Remember, the most important thing is to observe and understand your place.

Garden Layout and Sun Map

You can draw your backyard, garden or even your patio here. Don't worry too much about how precise your drawing is. Remember, the most important thing is to observe and understand your place.

Garden Layout and Sun Map

You can draw your backyard, garden or even your patio here. Don't worry too much about how precise your drawing is. Remember, the most important thing is to observe and understand your place.

A Moment of Joy - Picnic in My Garden

EEmbrace life's simple joys by turning your garden into a personal haven for relaxation. Enjoy a delightful picnic under your flourishing fruit trees, creating a peaceful escape on your property.

As you spread a blanket beneath the leafy canopy, take a moment to appreciate the beauty around you - the rustle of leaves, the sweet fragrance of blossoms, and the tunes of birds overhead.

Revel in the tranquility of your outdoor retreat, savoring the fruits of your gardening while appreciating the unique charm of your property.

A garden picnic is a delightful respite, reminding you to enjoy nature's simple pleasures in your own backyard.

DATE..

MY OBSERVATIONS:

....
....
....
....
....
....
....
....
....

THIS MADE ME FEEL:

Shrubs and Berries Bed Planner

Once you've identified your property's different zones and sun exposure areas, you can start designing your garden bed layouts.
One helpful approach is sketching your garden outline and experimenting with different plant arrangements for each area.

By considering factors like plant size, growth habits, and water needs, you can create a beautiful and functional garden that suits your property's unique characteristics.

Year: 2024

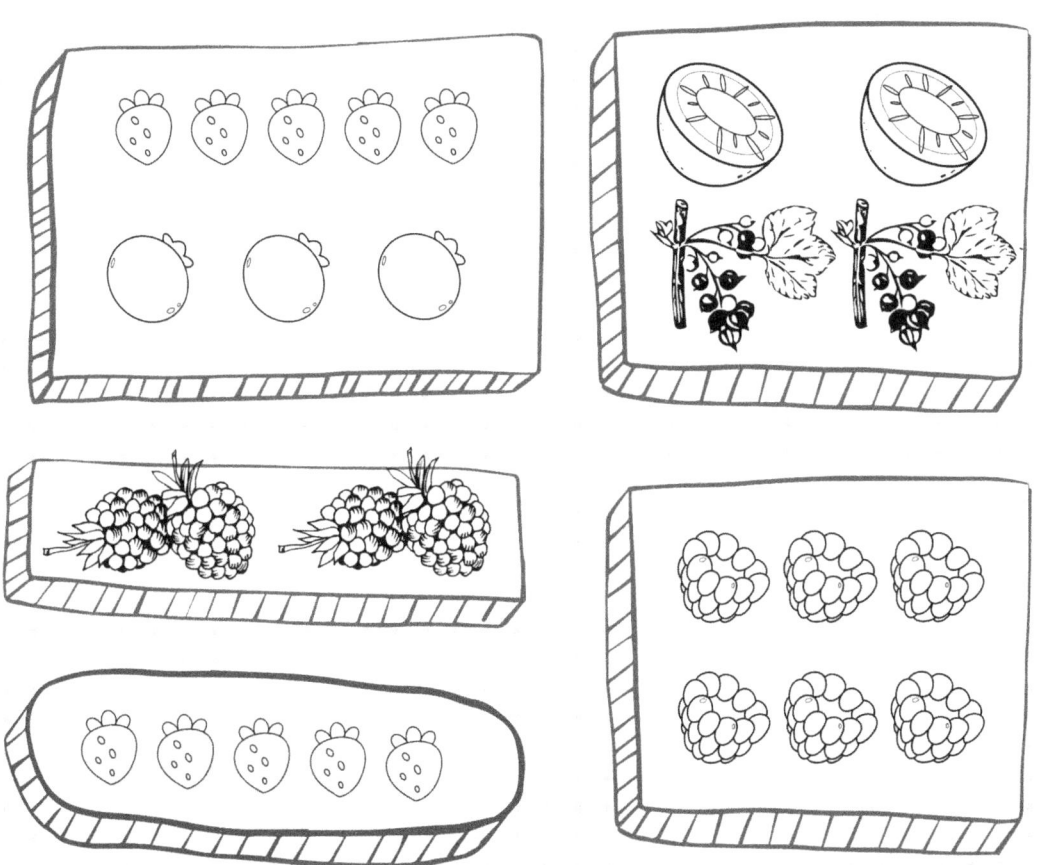

Shrubs and Berries Bed Planner

Year: Season:

Shrubs and Berries Bed Planner

Year: Season:

Garden Planner

Year: Season:

Garden Planner

Year: Season:

Tree Planting Log

Tree/Variant	Date Planted	Rootballed, Containerized, or Bare Root?	Additional Notes

Tree Planting Log

Tree/Variant	Date Planted	Rootballed, Containerized, or Bare Root?	Additional Notes

My Pruning Glossary

If you're new to growing trees, the different terminologies used for pruning may sound confusing. You will see below a tree and its various parts in relation to pruning. I've included a glossary of the tree parts that you're bound to encounter when you take up the shears.

Remember that some common words such as twig, shoot, limb, and branch are used interchangeably. However, a twig or a shoot is mostly used for young growth, while limb and branch are used for older, more mature growth.

- **Branch Collar:** Raised tissue at the bottom of each branch, containing specialized cells that protect pruning wounds from fungal infections.
- **Crotch Angle:** The angle between the tree trunk and a limb. The sharpest crotch angles range from 45 to 60 degrees.
- **Crown:** The base of the tree where the trunk meets the ground.
- **Head Cut/ Heading**: A pruning cut that takes out a specific part of a branch.
- **Lateral Branch:** The sideshoot of a branch, lying at a horizontal angle.
- **Leader:** The top most portion of a scaffold limb.
- **Scaffold Limb:** The largest branch serving as the foundation of a tree.
- **Shoot:** The length a branch achieves during one growing season.
- **Stub:** A small portion of a branch remaining after pruning, which should always be avoided.
- **Sucker Sprout:** A year old shoot growing from the root ball.
- **Terminal:** The portion where a shoot ends.
- **Thinning Cut:** A pruning cut that slices a branch from its point of origin. For example, in the image next page the branch requires more thinning toward the end marked with gray.
- **Vertical Branch:** A branch growing upright.
- **Water Sprout:** A year old shoot growing within a tree.

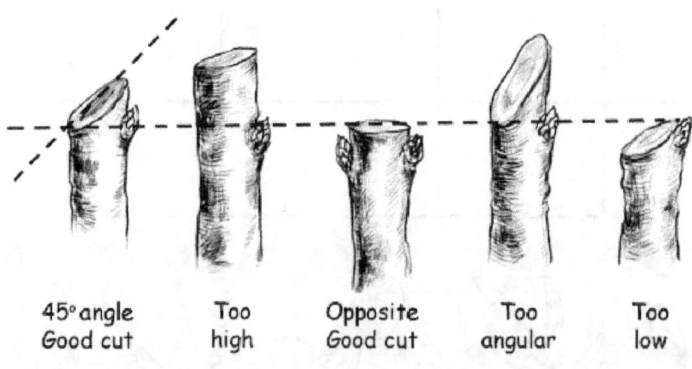

Pruning Basics

- Start by pruning all the fruit and nut trees so the tops are proportionate with the roots.
- Save heavy pruning for mature trees especially if they show slow growth.
- Prune the top more heavily than the lower branches.
- Prune after the early winter freeze has passed or during autumn.
- Thin out the shoots growing at the branch's end in mature trees to boost the size and quality of fruit.

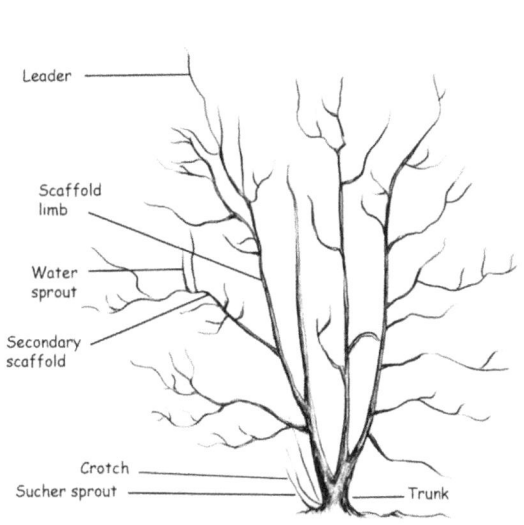

Common terms used in pruning and training fruit trees

On this well-developed branch, remove additional shoots towards the end

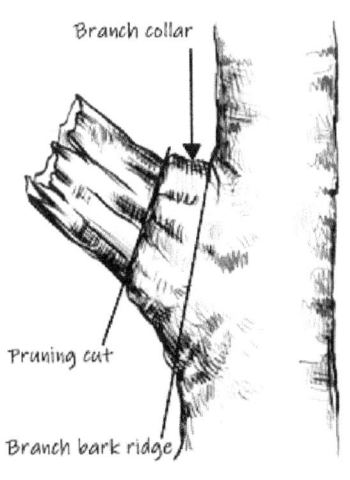

Heading cut
Pruning cuts in relationship to stem buds

Pruning Basics

- Start by pruning all the fruit and nut trees so the tops are proportionate with the roots.
- Save heavy pruning for mature trees, especially if they grow slowly.
- Prune the top more heavily than the lower branches.
- Prune after the early winter freeze has passed or during autumn.
- Thin out the shoots growing at the branch's end in mature trees to boost the size and quality of fruit.

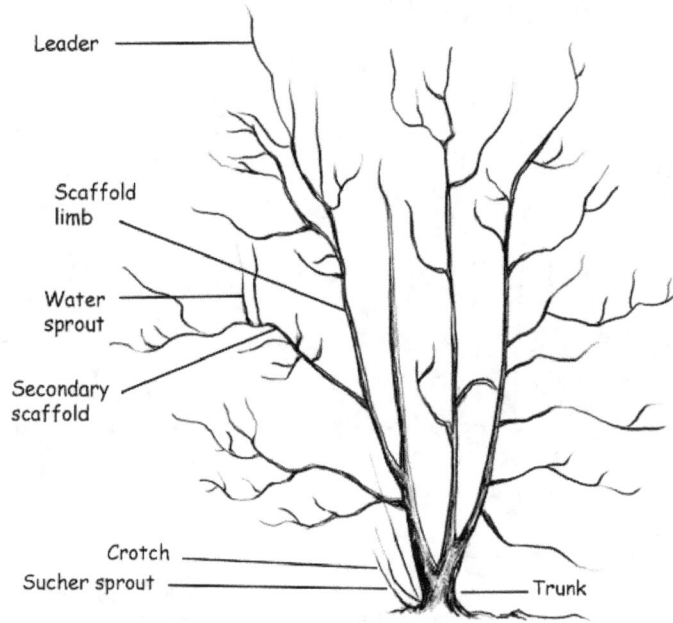

Common terms used in pruning and training fruit trees

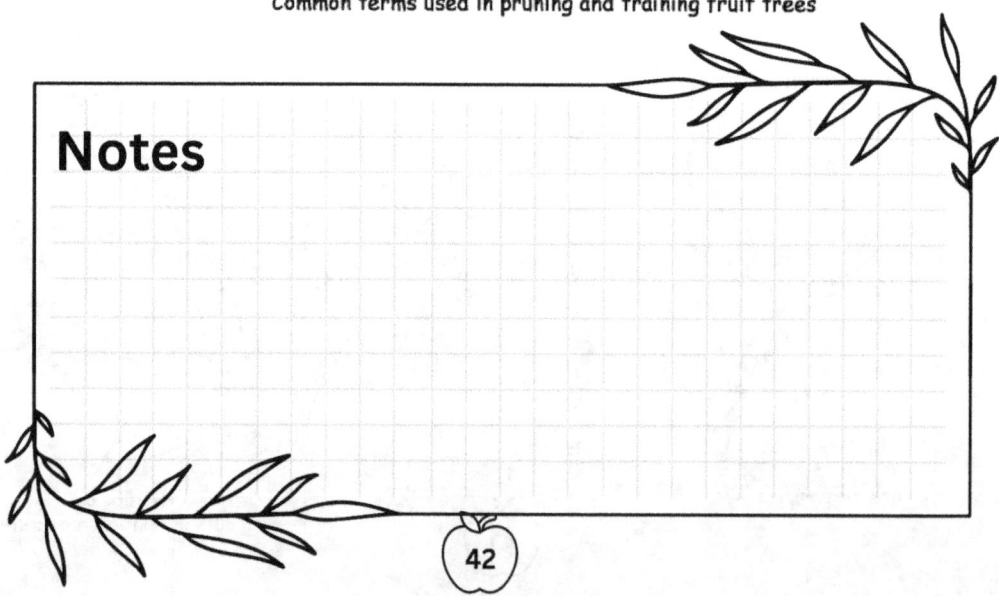

Notes

How to do the first spring and summer pruning?

The first spring after hard pruning your trees is crucial as this is when the tree breaks out of dormancy, budding below the pruning cuts. It doesn't take long for the top three or four buds to develop into scaffold branches by summer. Here are the steps you need to follow during the first spring and summer season:

1. **Cut down multiple leaf buds to one bud on each branch.** Use your fingers to snap multiple buds sprouting from a single leaf node, leaving behind only one. Do this around March or April then revisit the tree for more pruning in June.
2. **Remove the suckers from rootstocks.** Cut the limbs sprouting at or below the graft. Shoots coming out from the rootstock sap the plant's energy by redirecting resources away from the scion. Moreover, the branches emerging from the rootstocks don't produce decent fruit.
3. **Reconsider the current scaffold.** By early summer, young branches will begin assuming strength. Ideally, the top buds grow into well-formed scaffolds and the young tree develops three or four evenly spaced branches around the trunk. However, if the branches break or the top buds become inactive, you'll have to make a clean 45 degree prune near the top branching bud. The cut will become the crotch of the tree. You can take this moment to wonder if the cut you made was low enough and consider dropping the scaffold for shorter tree height and more lower branching. If the idea of a lower scaffold appeals to you, make another clean cut at a 45 degree angle.
4. **Think about the arrangement of future scaffold limbs.** Remove one or two branches growing too close to one another. Leave the shoots emerging above the graft even if they're low as they belong to the scion and will bear fruit. While pruning, keep angled branches and do away with limbs that are too horizontal or vertical. This is because at about 45 degrees, a branch is horizontal enough to bear fruit and angled enough to support its weight.
5. **Shorten the limbs.** Remove the extraneous branches, reducing the remaining branches at least half to a bud facing the direction you want the limb to grow.

Notes

Tree Pruning Log

Tree / Variant	Date of Pruning	Purpose of Pruning	Additional Notes

Tree Pruning Log

Tree / Variant	Date of Pruning	Purpose of Pruning	Additional Notes

Tree Pruning Log

Tree / Variant	Date of Pruning	Purpose of Pruning	Additional Notes

MY CALENDAR

JANUARY

FEBRUARY

MARCH

MY CALENDAR

JULY

AUGUST

SEPTEMBER

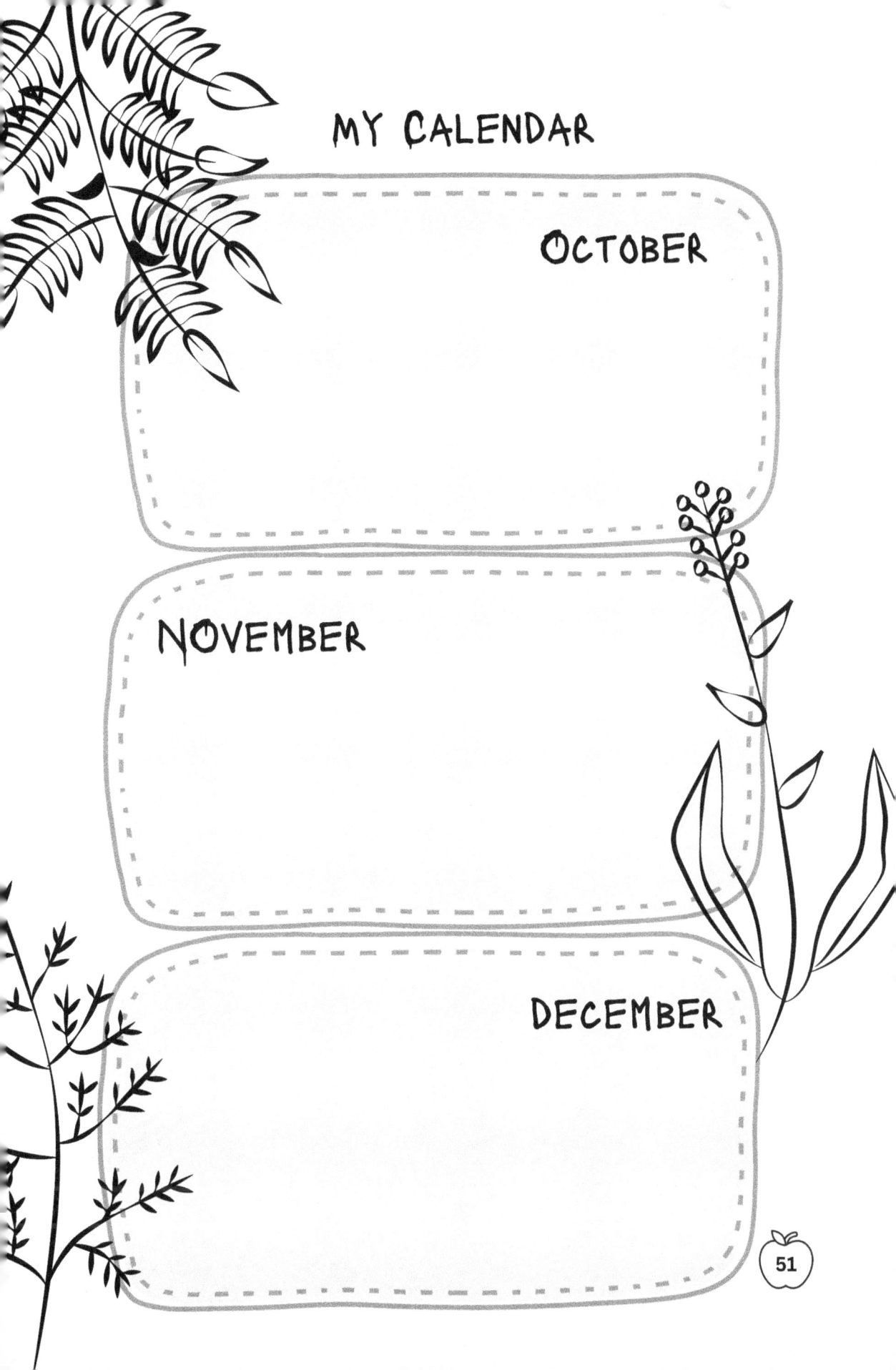

MY CALENDAR

OCTOBER

NOVEMBER

DECEMBER

MY CALENDAR

MY CALENDAR

MY CALENDAR

MY CALENDAR

Planting, Blooming, and Harvesting Timeline

A garden timeline is a great way to stay organized and motivated throughout the gardening season. You can start by marking your zone's first and last frost dates. Then, as the season goes on, note the key stages of your tree's life cycle, as well as the major tasks you need to do.

This could include planting, germination, transplanting, pruning, fertilizing, and harvesting. For each stage, note down the dates, and which tasks that needed to be done and when.

For example, if you're taking care of your fruit trees, you might include planting the trees in early spring, rejuvenating old trees, pruning, pest mangement, harvesting the ripe fruit in late summer etc.

You can draw, color, or simply make notes. Give it a try and see how it can transform your gardening experience!

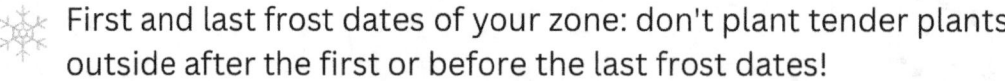

- First and last frost dates of your zone: don't plant tender plants outside after the first or before the last frost dates!
- Budding time
- Blooming: register the plant's blooming time
- Harvesting period: mark the harvest periods!
- Pruning: mark the best time for pruning!

Seasonal Chore Planner
My Early Spring Tasks

Months:

Fruit trees / Garden Beds
- [ ]
- [ ]
- [ ]
- [ ]
- [ ]
- [ ]
- [ ]
- [ ]
- [ ]

Pruning / Maintenance
- [ ]
- [ ]
- [ ]
- [ ]
- [ ]
- [ ]
- [ ]
- [ ]
- [ ]

Fertilizers
- [ ]
- [ ]
- [ ]
- [ ]
- [ ]
- [ ]
- [ ]
- [ ]
- [ ]

Planting/Harvesting
- [ ]
- [ ]
- [ ]
- [ ]
- [ ]
- [ ]
- [ ]
- [ ]
- [ ]

Seasonal Chore Planner
My Late Spring Tasks

- Months:

Fruit trees / Garden Beds

- [ ]
- [ ]
- [ ]
- [ ]
- [ ]
- [ ]
- [ ]
- [ ]
- [ ]

Pruning / Maintenance

- [ ]
- [ ]
- [ ]
- [ ]
- [ ]
- [ ]
- [ ]
- [ ]
- [ ]

Fertilizers

- [ ]
- [ ]
- [ ]
- [ ]
- [ ]
- [ ]
- [ ]
- [ ]
- [ ]

Planting/Harvesting

- [ ]
- [ ]
- [ ]
- [ ]
- [ ]
- [ ]
- [ ]
- [ ]
- [ ]

Seasonal Review: Spring

Plants harvested this season

Plants to try next season

What worked this season

What to do differently next season

Additional notes from this growing season

Seasonal Chore Planner
My Early Summer Tasks

Months:

Fruit trees / Garden Beds
- [ ]
- [ ]
- [ ]
- [ ]
- [ ]
- [ ]
- [ ]
- [ ]
- [ ]
- [ ]

Pruning / Maintenance
- [ ]
- [ ]
- [ ]
- [ ]
- [ ]
- [ ]
- [ ]
- [ ]
- [ ]
- [ ]

Fertilizers
- [ ]
- [ ]
- [ ]
- [ ]
- [ ]
- [ ]
- [ ]
- [ ]
- [ ]
- [ ]

Planting/Harvesting
- [ ]
- [ ]
- [ ]
- [ ]
- [ ]
- [ ]
- [ ]
- [ ]
- [ ]
- [ ]

Seasonal Chore Planner
My Late Summer Tasks

Months:

Fruit trees / Garden Beds
- [ ]
- [ ]
- [ ]
- [ ]
- [ ]
- [ ]
- [ ]
- [ ]
- [ ]

Pruning / Maintenance
- [ ]
- [ ]
- [ ]
- [ ]
- [ ]
- [ ]
- [ ]
- [ ]
- [ ]

Fertilizers
- [ ]
- [ ]
- [ ]
- [ ]
- [ ]
- [ ]
- [ ]
- [ ]
- [ ]

Planting/Harvesting
- [ ]
- [ ]
- [ ]
- [ ]
- [ ]
- [ ]
- [ ]
- [ ]
- [ ]

Seasonal Review: Summer

Plants harvested this season

Plants to try next season

What worked this season

What to do differently next season

Additional notes from this growing season

Seasonal Chore Planner
My Fall Tasks

Months:

Fruit trees / Garden Beds

- [ ]
- [ ]
- [ ]
- [ ]
- [ ]
- [ ]
- [ ]
- [ ]
- [ ]

Pruning / Maintenance

- [ ]
- [ ]
- [ ]
- [ ]
- [ ]
- [ ]
- [ ]
- [ ]
- [ ]

Fertilizers

- [ ]
- [ ]
- [ ]
- [ ]
- [ ]
- [ ]
- [ ]
- [ ]
- [ ]

Planting/Harvesting

- [ ]
- [ ]
- [ ]
- [ ]
- [ ]
- [ ]
- [ ]
- [ ]
- [ ]

Seasonal review: Fall

Plants harvested this season

Plants to try next season

What worked this season

What to do differently next season

Additional notes from this growing season

Seasonal Chore Planner
My Winter Tasks

Months:

Fruit trees / Garden Beds

- [ ]
- [ ]
- [ ]
- [ ]
- [ ]
- [ ]
- [ ]
- [ ]
- [ ]

Pruning / Maintenance

- [ ]
- [ ]
- [ ]
- [ ]
- [ ]
- [ ]
- [ ]
- [ ]
- [ ]

Fertilizers

- [ ]
- [ ]
- [ ]
- [ ]
- [ ]
- [ ]
- [ ]
- [ ]
- [ ]

Planting/Harvesting

- [ ]
- [ ]
- [ ]
- [ ]
- [ ]
- [ ]
- [ ]
- [ ]
- [ ]

Seasonal review: Winter

Plants harvested this season

Plants to try next season

What worked this season

What to do differently next season

Additional notes from this growing season

Bringing old trees to life

Old, forgotten trees tend to become home for insects and diseases, which can spread to other trees. If you've resolved to restore your old fruit tree, here are the steps you should take:

1. Perform a heavy, corrective prune when the tree is dormant.
2. Reshape the tree during the first year. Shorten it by 6 to 8 feet, if it's over 20 feet tall.
3. Cut the main scaffold limbs.
4. Prune the upper third of the tree, getting rid of dead, crossing, and hanging branches.
5. Remove vigorous top shoots during the summer of the following year.
6. Leave a few minor branches at the lower part of the trunk that don't provide too much shade. This will encourage the tree to produce new fruit wood.
7. Cut down half of the new branches on the top in the third year. Look for shoots growing near the previous heavy pruning cuts.
8. Remove the strongest shoots first.
9. Shape the tree during the 3rd dormant period and shorten it by 1 or 2 feet.
10. Spread the newly formed wood, making sure all the branches are easily accessible for pruning, spraying, and harvesting.

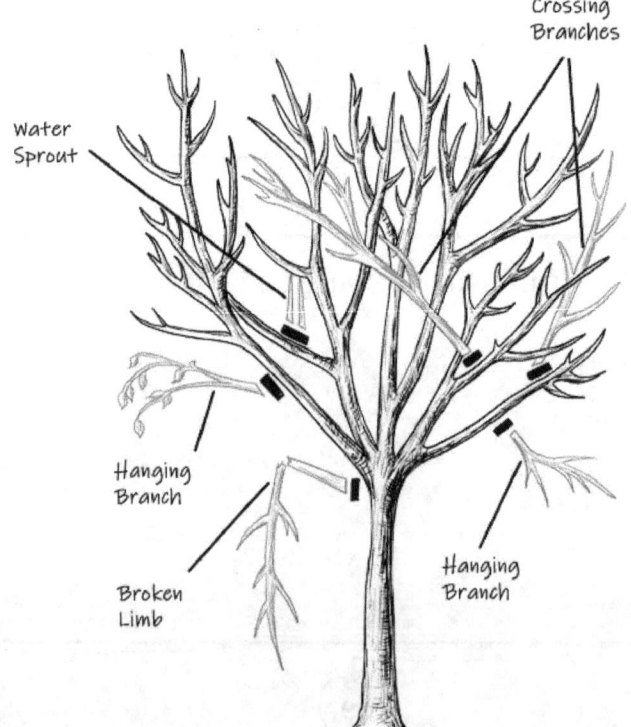

Tree Rejuvenating Action Plan

Tree / Variant	Date and Location	Action	Additional Notes

Tree Rejuvenating Action Plan

Tree / Variant	Date and Location	Action	Additional Notes

Notes

KEEP BUGS AWAY PLANT THESE

- **BASIL**: mosquitoes + flies
- **CATNIP**: mosquitoes
- **LAVENDER**: mosquitoes, flies, moths + fleas
- **MARIGOLDS**: mosquitoes + aphids
- **PEPPERMINT**: mosquitoes, ants + spiders
- **ROSEMARY**: fleas, ticks, mosquitoes + slugs
- **SAGE**: moths

Notes

Tree / Plant Profiles

PLANT NAME ....

FRUIT ☐ TREE ☐ SHRUB ☐ SEEDLING ☐ GRAFTED ☐ CONTAINERED ☐ TRAINED ☐
VEGETABLE ☐ HERB ☐ FLOWER ☐ ANNUAL ☐ BIENNIAL ☐ PERENNIAL ☐

Plant source	
Purchase date	
Cost	

TIMETABLE	
GERMINATION DATE	
PLANTING DATE	
TRANSPLANT DATE	
BLOOM DATE	
HARVEST DATE	
HARVEST TOTAL	
SEED SAVING DATE	
PRUNING DATE	

PLANT NEEDS	
LOCATION	
SUN	☀ ☀ ☀ ☀ ☀
WATER NEED	💧 💧 💧 💧 💧
HUMIDITY	
FERTILIZERS	
SOIL AMENDMENT	
RATE YOUR PLANT	🍃 🍃 🍃 🍃 🍃

NOTES

....
....
....
....
....
....

PESTS - WEEDS - DISEASES - SOLUTIONS

Tree / Plant Profiles

PLANT NAME ....

FRUIT ☐ TREE ☐ SHRUB ☐ SEEDLING ☐ GRAFTED ☐ CONTAINERED ☐ TRAINED ☐ VEGETABLE ☐ HERB ☐ FLOWER ☐ ANNUAL ☐ BIENNIAL ☐ PERENNIAL ☐	
Plant source	
Purchase date	
Cost	

TIMETABLE	
GERMINATION DATE	
PLANTING DATE	
TRANSPLANT DATE	
BLOOM DATE	
HARVEST DATE	
HARVEST TOTAL	
SEED SAVING DATE	
PRUNING DATE	

PLANT NEEDS	
LOCATION	
SUN	☼ ☼ ☼ ☼ ☼
WATER NEED	💧 💧 💧 💧 💧
HUMIDITY	
FERTILIZERS	
SOIL AMENDMENT	
RATE YOUR PLANT	🍃 🍃 🍃 🍃 🍃

NOTES

....
....
....
....
....
....
....

PESTS - WEEDS - DISEASES - SOLUTIONS

Tree / Plant Profiles

PLANT NAME ....

FRUIT ☐   TREE ☐   SHRUB ☐   SEEDLING ☐   GRAFTED ☐   CONTAINERED ☐   TRAINED ☐ VEGETABLE ☐   HERB ☐   FLOWER ☐   ANNUAL ☐   BIENNIAL ☐   PERENNIAL ☐
Plant source
Purchase date
Cost

TIMETABLE

GERMINATION DATE	
PLANTING DATE	
TRANSPLANT DATE	
BLOOM DATE	
HARVEST DATE	
HARVEST TOTAL	
SEED SAVING DATE	
PRUNING DATE	

PLANT NEEDS

LOCATION	
SUN	☀ ☀ ☀ ☀ ☀
WATER NEED	💧 💧 💧 💧 💧
HUMIDITY	
FERTILIZERS	
SOIL AMENDMENT	
RATE YOUR PLANT	🍃 🍃 🍃 🍃 🍃

NOTES
....
....
....
....
....
....
....

PESTS - WEEDS - DISEASES - SOLUTIONS

Tree / Plant Profiles

PLANT NAME ....

FRUIT ☐ TREE ☐ SHRUB ☐ SEEDLING ☐ GRAFTED ☐ CONTAINERED ☐ TRAINED ☐
VEGETABLE ☐ HERB ☐ FLOWER ☐ ANNUAL ☐ BIENNIAL ☐ PERENNIAL ☐

Plant source	
Purchase date	
Cost	

TIMETABLE

GERMINATION DATE	
PLANTING DATE	
TRANSPLANT DATE	
BLOOM DATE	
HARVEST DATE	
HARVEST TOTAL	
SEED SAVING DATE	
PRUNING DATE	

PLANT NEEDS

LOCATION	
SUN	☀ ☀ ☀ ☀ ☀
WATER NEED	💧 💧 💧 💧 💧
HUMIDITY	
FERTILIZERS	
SOIL AMENDMENT	
RATE YOUR PLANT	🍃 🍃 🍃 🍃 🍃

NOTES

....
....
....
....
....
....
....

PESTS - WEEDS - DISEASES - SOLUTIONS

Tree / Plant Profiles

PLANT NAME ....

FRUIT ☐   TREE ☐   SHRUB ☐   SEEDLING ☐   GRAFTED ☐   CONTAINERED ☐   TRAINED ☐
VEGETABLE ☐   HERB ☐   FLOWER ☐   ANNUAL ☐   BIENNIAL ☐   PERENNIAL ☐

Plant source	
Purchase date	
Cost	

TIMETABLE

GERMINATION DATE	
PLANTING DATE	
TRANSPLANT DATE	
BLOOM DATE	
HARVEST DATE	
HARVEST TOTAL	
SEED SAVING DATE	
PRUNING DATE	

PLANT NEEDS

LOCATION	
SUN	☀ ☀ ☀ ☀ ☀
WATER NEED	💧 💧 💧 💧 💧
HUMIDITY	
FERTILIZERS	
SOIL AMENDMENT	
RATE YOUR PLANT	🍃 🍃 🍃 🍃 🍃

NOTES

....
....
....
....
....
....
....

PESTS – WEEDS – DISEASES – SOLUTIONS

Tree / Plant Profiles

PLANT NAME ....

FRUIT ☐   TREE ☐   SHRUB ☐   SEEDLING ☐   GRAFTED ☐   CONTAINERED ☐   TRAINED ☐
VEGETABLE ☐   HERB ☐   FLOWER ☐   ANNUAL ☐   BIENNIAL ☐   PERENNIAL ☐

Plant source	
Purchase date	
Cost	

TIMETABLE

GERMINATION DATE	
PLANTING DATE	
TRANSPLANT DATE	
BLOOM DATE	
HARVEST DATE	
HARVEST TOTAL	
SEED SAVING DATE	
PRUNING DATE	

PLANT NEEDS

LOCATION	
SUN	☀ ☀ ☀ ☀ ☀
WATER NEED	💧 💧 💧 💧 💧
HUMIDITY	
FERTILIZERS	
SOIL AMENDMENT	
RATE YOUR PLANT	🍃 🍃 🍃 🍃 🍃

NOTES

....
....
....
....
....
....
....

PESTS - WEEDS - DISEASES - SOLUTIONS

Tree / Plant Profiles

PLANT NAME ....

FRUIT ☐ TREE ☐ SHRUB ☐ SEEDLING ☐ GRAFTED ☐ CONTAINERED ☐ TRAINED ☐
VEGETABLE ☐ HERB ☐ FLOWER ☐ ANNUAL ☐ BIENNIAL ☐ PERENNIAL ☐

Plant source	
Purchase date	
Cost	

TIMETABLE

GERMINATION DATE	
PLANTING DATE	
TRANSPLANT DATE	
BLOOM DATE	
HARVEST DATE	
HARVEST TOTAL	
SEED SAVING DATE	
PRUNING DATE	

PLANT NEEDS

LOCATION	
SUN	☀ ☀ ☀ ☀ ☀
WATER NEED	💧 💧 💧 💧 💧
HUMIDITY	
FERTILIZERS	
SOIL AMENDMENT	
RATE YOUR PLANT	🍃 🍃 🍃 🍃 🍃

NOTES

....
....
....
....
....
....
....

PESTS - WEEDS - DISEASES - SOLUTIONS

Tree / Plant Profiles

PLANT NAME ....

| FRUIT ☐   TREE ☐   SHRUB ☐   SEEDLING ☐   GRAFTED ☐   CONTAINERED ☐   TRAINED ☐ |
| VEGETABLE ☐   HERB ☐   FLOWER ☐   ANNUAL ☐   BIENNIAL ☐   PERENNIAL ☐ |

Plant source	
Purchase date	
Cost	

TIMETABLE

GERMINATION DATE	
PLANTING DATE	
TRANSPLANT DATE	
BLOOM DATE	
HARVEST DATE	
HARVEST TOTAL	
SEED SAVING DATE	
PRUNING DATE	

PLANT NEEDS

LOCATION	
SUN	☀ ☀ ☀ ☀ ☀
WATER NEED	💧 💧 💧 💧 💧
HUMIDITY	
FERTILIZERS	
SOIL AMENDMENT	
RATE YOUR PLANT	🍃 🍃 🍃 🍃 🍃

NOTES

....
....
....
....
....
....
....

PESTS - WEEDS - DISEASES - SOLUTIONS

Tree / Plant Profiles

PLANT NAME ....

| FRUIT ☐ TREE ☐ SHRUB ☐ SEEDLING ☐ GRAFTED ☐ CONTAINERED ☐ TRAINED ☐ |
| VEGETABLE ☐ HERB ☐ FLOWER ☐ ANNUAL ☐ BIENNIAL ☐ PERENNIAL ☐ |

Plant source	
Purchase date	
Cost	

TIMETABLE

GERMINATION DATE	
PLANTING DATE	
TRANSPLANT DATE	
BLOOM DATE	
HARVEST DATE	
HARVEST TOTAL	
SEED SAVING DATE	
PRUNING DATE	

PLANT NEEDS

LOCATION	
SUN	☼ ☼ ☼ ☼ ☼
WATER NEED	💧 💧 💧 💧 💧
HUMIDITY	
FERTILIZERS	
SOIL AMENDMENT	
RATE YOUR PLANT	🍃 🍃 🍃 🍃 🍃

NOTES

....
....
....
....
....
....

PESTS – WEEDS – DISEASES – SOLUTIONS

Tree / Plant Profiles

PLANT NAME ....

| FRUIT ☐ TREE ☐ SHRUB ☐ SEEDLING ☐ GRAFTED ☐ CONTAINERED ☐ TRAINED ☐ |
| VEGETABLE ☐ HERB ☐ FLOWER ☐ ANNUAL ☐ BIENNIAL ☐ PERENNIAL ☐ |

Plant source	
Purchase date	
Cost	

TIMETABLE

GERMINATION DATE	
PLANTING DATE	
TRANSPLANT DATE	
BLOOM DATE	
HARVEST DATE	
HARVEST TOTAL	
SEED SAVING DATE	
PRUNING DATE	

PLANT NEEDS

LOCATION	
SUN	☼ ☼ ☼ ☼ ☼
WATER NEED	💧 💧 💧 💧 💧
HUMIDITY	
FERTILIZERS	
SOIL AMENDMENT	
RATE YOUR PLANT	🍃 🍃 🍃 🍃 🍃

NOTES

....
....
....
....
....
....
....

PESTS - WEEDS - DISEASES - SOLUTIONS

Tree / Plant Profiles

PLANT NAME ....

FRUIT ☐ TREE ☐ SHRUB ☐ SEEDLING ☐ GRAFTED ☐ CONTAINERED ☐ TRAINED ☐
VEGETABLE ☐ HERB ☐ FLOWER ☐ ANNUAL ☐ BIENNIAL ☐ PERENNIAL ☐

Plant source	
Purchase date	
Cost	

TIMETABLE

GERMINATION DATE	
PLANTING DATE	
TRANSPLANT DATE	
BLOOM DATE	
HARVEST DATE	
HARVEST TOTAL	
SEED SAVING DATE	
PRUNING DATE	

PLANT NEEDS

LOCATION	
SUN	☀ ☀ ☀ ☀ ☀
WATER NEED	💧 💧 💧 💧 💧
HUMIDITY	
FERTILIZERS	
SOIL AMENDMENT	
RATE YOUR PLANT	🍃 🍃 🍃 🍃 🍃

NOTES

....
....
....
....
....
....
....

PESTS - WEEDS - DISEASES - SOLUTIONS

Tree / Plant Profiles

PLANT NAME ....

| FRUIT ☐ TREE ☐ SHRUB ☐ SEEDLING ☐ GRAFTED ☐ CONTAINERED ☐ TRAINED ☐ |
| VEGETABLE ☐ HERB ☐ FLOWER ☐ ANNUAL ☐ BIENNIAL ☐ PERENNIAL ☐ |

Plant source	
Purchase date	
Cost	

TIMETABLE

GERMINATION DATE	
PLANTING DATE	
TRANSPLANT DATE	
BLOOM DATE	
HARVEST DATE	
HARVEST TOTAL	
SEED SAVING DATE	
PRUNING DATE	

PLANT NEEDS

LOCATION	
SUN	☀ ☀ ☀ ☀ ☀
WATER NEED	💧 💧 💧 💧 💧
HUMIDITY	
FERTILIZERS	
SOIL AMENDMENT	
RATE YOUR PLANT	🍃 🍃 🍃 🍃 🍃

NOTES

....
....
....
....
....
....
....

PESTS - WEEDS - DISEASES - SOLUTIONS

Tree / Plant Profiles

PLANT NAME ....

| FRUIT ☐ TREE ☐ SHRUB ☐ SEEDLING ☐ GRAFTED ☐ CONTAINERED ☐ TRAINED ☐ |
| VEGETABLE ☐ HERB ☐ FLOWER ☐ ANNUAL ☐ BIENNIAL ☐ PERENNIAL ☐ |

Plant source	
Purchase date	
Cost	

TIMETABLE

GERMINATION DATE	
PLANTING DATE	
TRANSPLANT DATE	
BLOOM DATE	
HARVEST DATE	
HARVEST TOTAL	
SEED SAVING DATE	
PRUNING DATE	

PLANT NEEDS

LOCATION	
SUN	☼ ☼ ☼ ☼ ☼
WATER NEED	💧 💧 💧 💧 💧
HUMIDITY	
FERTILIZERS	
SOIL AMENDMENT	
RATE YOUR PLANT	🍃 🍃 🍃 🍃 🍃

NOTES

....
....
....
....
....
....

PESTS - WEEDS - DISEASES - SOLUTIONS

Tree / Plant Profiles

PLANT NAME ....

FRUIT ☐   TREE ☐   SHRUB ☐   SEEDLING ☐   GRAFTED ☐   CONTAINERED ☐   TRAINED ☐ VEGETABLE ☐   HERB ☐   FLOWER ☐   ANNUAL ☐   BIENNIAL ☐   PERENNIAL ☐
Plant source
Purchase date
Cost

TIMETABLE	
GERMINATION DATE	
PLANTING DATE	
TRANSPLANT DATE	
BLOOM DATE	
HARVEST DATE	
HARVEST TOTAL	
SEED SAVING DATE	
PRUNING DATE	

PLANT NEEDS	
LOCATION	
SUN	☼ ☼ ☼ ☼ ☼
WATER NEED	💧 💧 💧 💧 💧
HUMIDITY	
FERTILIZERS	
SOIL AMENDMENT	
RATE YOUR PLANT	🍃 🍃 🍃 🍃 🍃

NOTES

....
....
....
....
....
....
....

PESTS - WEEDS - DISEASES - SOLUTIONS

Tree / Plant Profiles

PLANT NAME ....

FRUIT ☐ TREE ☐ SHRUB ☐ SEEDLING ☐ GRAFTED ☐ CONTAINERED ☐ TRAINED ☐
VEGETABLE ☐ HERB ☐ FLOWER ☐ ANNUAL ☐ BIENNIAL ☐ PERENNIAL ☐

Plant source	
Purchase date	
Cost	

TIMETABLE

GERMINATION DATE	
PLANTING DATE	
TRANSPLANT DATE	
BLOOM DATE	
HARVEST DATE	
HARVEST TOTAL	
SEED SAVING DATE	
PRUNING DATE	

PLANT NEEDS

LOCATION	
SUN	☀ ☀ ☀ ☀ ☀
WATER NEED	💧 💧 💧 💧 💧
HUMIDITY	
FERTILIZERS	
SOIL AMENDMENT	
RATE YOUR PLANT	🍃 🍃 🍃 🍃 🍃

NOTES

....
....
....
....
....
....
....

PESTS - WEEDS - DISEASES - SOLUTIONS

Tree / Plant Profiles

PLANT NAME ....

| FRUIT ☐ TREE ☐ SHRUB ☐ SEEDLING ☐ GRAFTED ☐ CONTAINERED ☐ TRAINED ☐ |
| VEGETABLE ☐ HERB ☐ FLOWER ☐ ANNUAL ☐ BIENNIAL ☐ PERENNIAL ☐ |

Plant source	
Purchase date	
Cost	

TIMETABLE	
GERMINATION DATE	
PLANTING DATE	
TRANSPLANT DATE	
BLOOM DATE	
HARVEST DATE	
HARVEST TOTAL	
SEED SAVING DATE	
PRUNING DATE	

PLANT NEEDS	
LOCATION	
SUN	☀ ☀ ☀ ☀ ☀
WATER NEED	💧 💧 💧 💧 💧
HUMIDITY	
FERTILIZERS	
SOIL AMENDMENT	
RATE YOUR PLANT	🍃 🍃 🍃 🍃 🍃

NOTES

....
....
....
....
....
....
....

PESTS - WEEDS - DISEASES - SOLUTIONS

Tree / Plant Profiles

PLANT NAME ....

FRUIT ☐ TREE ☐ SHRUB ☐ SEEDLING ☐ GRAFTED ☐ CONTAINERED ☐ TRAINED ☐ VEGETABLE ☐ HERB ☐ FLOWER ☐ ANNUAL ☐ BIENNIAL ☐ PERENNIAL ☐	
Plant source	
Purchase date	
Cost	

TIMETABLE

GERMINATION DATE	
PLANTING DATE	
TRANSPLANT DATE	
BLOOM DATE	
HARVEST DATE	
HARVEST TOTAL	
SEED SAVING DATE	
PRUNING DATE	

PLANT NEEDS

LOCATION	
SUN	☼ ☼ ☼ ☼ ☼
WATER NEED	💧 💧 💧 💧 💧
HUMIDITY	
FERTILIZERS	
SOIL AMENDMENT	
RATE YOUR PLANT	🍃 🍃 🍃 🍃 🍃

NOTES
....
....
....
....
....
....
....

PESTS - WEEDS - DISEASES - SOLUTIONS

Tree / Plant Profiles

PLANT NAME ....

| FRUIT ☐ TREE ☐ SHRUB ☐ SEEDLING ☐ GRAFTED ☐ CONTAINERED ☐ TRAINED ☐ |
| VEGETABLE ☐ HERB ☐ FLOWER ☐ ANNUAL ☐ BIENNIAL ☐ PERENNIAL ☐ |

Plant source	
Purchase date	
Cost	

TIMETABLE

GERMINATION DATE	
PLANTING DATE	
TRANSPLANT DATE	
BLOOM DATE	
HARVEST DATE	
HARVEST TOTAL	
SEED SAVING DATE	
PRUNING DATE	

PLANT NEEDS

LOCATION	
SUN	☼ ☼ ☼ ☼ ☼
WATER NEED	💧 💧 💧 💧 💧
HUMIDITY	
FERTILIZERS	
SOIL AMENDMENT	
RATE YOUR PLANT	🍃 🍃 🍃 🍃 🍃

NOTES

....
....
....
....
....
....
....

PESTS - WEEDS - DISEASES - SOLUTIONS

Tree / Plant Profiles

PLANT NAME ....

FRUIT ☐ TREE ☐ SHRUB ☐ SEEDLING ☐ GRAFTED ☐ CONTAINERED ☐ TRAINED ☐
VEGETABLE ☐ HERB ☐ FLOWER ☐ ANNUAL ☐ BIENNIAL ☐ PERENNIAL ☐

Plant source	
Purchase date	
Cost	

TIMETABLE

GERMINATION DATE	
PLANTING DATE	
TRANSPLANT DATE	
BLOOM DATE	
HARVEST DATE	
HARVEST TOTAL	
SEED SAVING DATE	
PRUNING DATE	

PLANT NEEDS

LOCATION	
SUN	☀ ☀ ☀ ☀ ☀
WATER NEED	💧 💧 💧 💧 💧
HUMIDITY	
FERTILIZERS	
SOIL AMENDMENT	
RATE YOUR PLANT	🍃 🍃 🍃 🍃 🍃

NOTES

....
....
....
....
....
....
....

PESTS – WEEDS – DISEASES – SOLUTIONS

Tree / Plant Profiles

PLANT NAME ....

| FRUIT ☐ TREE ☐ SHRUB ☐ SEEDLING ☐ GRAFTED ☐ CONTAINERED ☐ TRAINED ☐ |
| VEGETABLE ☐ HERB ☐ FLOWER ☐ ANNUAL ☐ BIENNIAL ☐ PERENNIAL ☐ |

Plant source	
Purchase date	
Cost	

TIMETABLE

GERMINATION DATE	
PLANTING DATE	
TRANSPLANT DATE	
BLOOM DATE	
HARVEST DATE	
HARVEST TOTAL	
SEED SAVING DATE	
PRUNING DATE	

PLANT NEEDS

LOCATION	
SUN	☀ ☀ ☀ ☀ ☀
WATER NEED	💧 💧 💧 💧 💧
HUMIDITY	
FERTILIZERS	
SOIL AMENDMENT	
RATE YOUR PLANT	🍃 🍃 🍃 🍃 🍃

NOTES

....
....
....
....
....
....

PESTS - WEEDS - DISEASES - SOLUTIONS

Composting Basics

Composting is the process of turning organic waste into nutrient-rich compost, which can be used to improve soil fertility and support healthy plant growth.

To start composting, **collect a mix of "green" materials and "brown" materials.** Layer these materials in a compost bin or pile, ensuring a good mix of carbon-rich browns and nitrogen-rich greens. It's important to maintain a moist (but not soggy) compost pile, regularly turning or aerating it to provide oxygen for the decomposition process.

As the materials break down, beneficial microorganisms and earthworms will naturally decompose the organic matter, turning it into nutrient-rich compost.

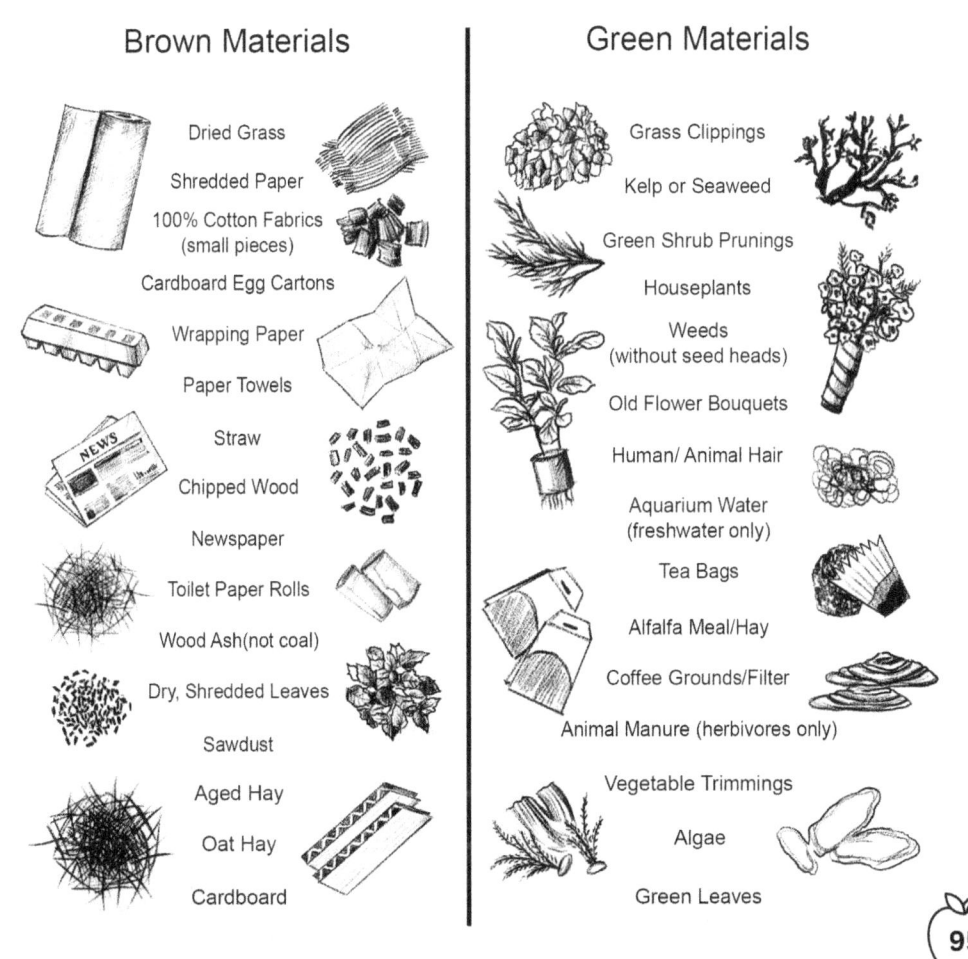

Browns & Greens
Sources for Compost

Brown Materials	Green Materials
Dried Grass	Grass Clippings
Shredded Paper	Kelp or Seaweed
100% Cotton Fabrics (small pieces)	Green Shrub Prunings
Cardboard Egg Cartons	Houseplants
Wrapping Paper	Weeds (without seed heads)
Paper Towels	Old Flower Bouquets
Straw	Human/ Animal Hair
Chipped Wood	Aquarium Water (freshwater only)
Newspaper	Tea Bags
Toilet Paper Rolls	Alfalfa Meal/Hay
Wood Ash(not coal)	Coffee Grounds/Filter
Dry, Shredded Leaves	Animal Manure (herbivores only)
Sawdust	Vegetable Trimmings
Aged Hay	Algae
Oat Hay	Green Leaves
Cardboard	

Notes

Rainfall Recording Sheet and Watering Tracker

Track the amount of rainfall by noting the measurements from your rain gauge or referring to official weather reports for your area. Document your watering activities as well.

Week	Monday	Tuesday	Wednesday	Thursday	Friday	Saturday	Sunday	Total for the week

Rainfall Recording Sheet and Watering Tracker

Track the amount of rainfall by noting the measurements from your rain gauge or referring to official weather reports for your area. Document your watering activities as well.

Week	Monday	Tuesday	Wednesday	Thursday	Friday	Saturday	Sunday	Total for the week

Rainfall Recording Sheet and Watering Tracker

Track the amount of rainfall by noting the measurements from your rain gauge or referring to official weather reports for your area. Document your watering activities as well.

Week	Monday	Tuesday	Wednesday	Thursday	Friday	Saturday	Sunday	Total for the week

Rainfall Recording Sheet and Watering Tracker

Track the amount of rainfall by noting the measurements from your rain gauge or referring to official weather reports for your area. Document your watering activities as well.

Week	Monday	Tuesday	Wednesday	Thursday	Friday	Saturday	Sunday	Total for the week

Water Saving Ideas for the Future

Pest and Disease Tracker

Healthy plants are strong enough to ward off potential problems. By fulfilling your plants' essential requirements, choosing varieties suited to your climate, and nipping problems in the bud, you can create an orchard that self-corrects.

When it comes to choosing chemical controls, it's best to try out the least toxic option first. This can be something as simple as handpicking the pests or insects, if possible.

Whenever you notice signs of pests or diseases in your garden, note the date and the specific symptoms or damage observed. Be detailed in your descriptions, noting the affected trees/plants, the specific parts of the plant impacted, and any distinctive characteristics of the pest or disease.

Note any treatments, interventions, sprays or organic remedies you apply, along with the date of each action. Monitor the progress and effectiveness of your treatments or interventions.
Make additional notes over time, recording any changes in the severity of the problem or improvements in the plant's health.

Pest / Disease	Trees/Plants affected	Problem	Treatment	Results

Pest and Disease Tracker

List any signs of pests or diseases observed, and note any action taken.

Pest / Disease	Plants affected	Problem	Treatment	Results

Pest and Disease Tracker

List any signs of pests or diseases observed, and note any action taken.

Pest / Disease	Plants affected	Problem	Treatment	Results

Pest and Disease Tracker

List any signs of pests or diseases observed, and note any action taken.

Pest / Disease	Plants affected	Problem	Treatment	Results

Bring the Bees to the Yard

Pollination is essential for the development of fruits. Without pollination, there will be no fruits to harvest. It involves the transfer of pollen from the stamen to the pistil. This leads to fertilization and the development of seeds. The honey bees, butterflies, bugs and hummingbirds that may wander into your orchard are essential to making all that happen!

Based on pollination, fruit trees can be sorted into two categories.
- **Self-Pollinating:** Trees that don't require other tree varieties to achieve pollination. These include apricots, peaches, sour cherries, and peaches.
- **Cross-Pollinating:** Trees that require another tree variety for pollination. Fruit trees such as pear, plums, and sweet cherries fall in this category.

To ensure effective pollination, it's best to plant at least two compatible pollen varieties within a hundred feet of each other. Make sure that the trees you choose bloom in the same season. Timing is everything for successful pollination. Early-season trees will pollinate other early season trees. The same principle applies to mid or late-season varieties.

FRUIT TREE	POLLENIZER REQUIRED	POLLINATORS	SELF-POLLINATION VARIETIES
Apple	most varieties	insects, especially honeybees	Ein Shemer, Gala, Golden Delicious, Dorsett Golden, Anna
Banana	no	none required	All
Cherry	some varieties	insects, especially honeybees	Benton, Blackgold, Lapins, Starkrimso, Stella, Whitegold, Tart Cherries
Fig	no	none required	All
Olive	some varieties	various insects	Arbequina
Peach	some varieties	various insects	FlordaCrest
Pear	yes	insects, especially honeybees	Kieffer, Shinseiki, Gulf Crimson, Pineapple Pear
Pecan	yes	the wind	Self-pollination is minimal and generally does not produce good quality nuts.
Persimmon	yes, a male tree	insects, especially honeybees	Asian Kaki Persimmons, Fuyu
Plum	most	insects, especially honeybees	Au Rosa, Golden, Methley, Santa Rosa, Scarlet Beauty
Pomegranate	no	insects, especially honeybees	All

Pollinator Fan Page

When you see pollinators such as bees, butterflies or hummingbirds, note the date, the type of pollinator, and any specific observations about their behavior or preferences.

Keep track of the steps you take to invite and support pollinators in your garden. These might include planting pollinator-friendly flowers, providing water sources, or creating habitat features such as nesting sites or insect hotels.

Use the pollinator fan page to learn from their experiences. Identify which plants, features, or practices are most successful in attracting and supporting pollinators. Use this knowledge to further enhance your garden as a pollinator-friendly place.

Name: *Honeybees*
Date: *May*
Where: *Grandma's orchard flower bed*
Notes: *They love lavenders!*

Name:
Date:
Where:
Notes:

Actions & results:
- We need more pollinator-friendly flowers next year
- Remember to provide fresh water for the birds & pollinators at the apple tree area

Pollinator Fan Page

Name: .... Date: ....
Where: .... Notes: ....
....
....
....

Name: .... Date: ....
Where: .... Notes: ....
....
....
....

Name: .... Date: ....
Where: .... Notes: ....
....
....
....

Name: .... Date: ....
Where: .... Notes: ....
....
....
....

Pollinator Fan Page

Name: .... Date: ....
Where: .... Notes: ....
....
....
....

Name: .... Date: ....
Where: .... Notes: ....
....
....
....

Name: .... Date: ....
Where: .... Notes: ....
....
....
....

Actions & results:

Pollinator Fan Page

Name: .... Date: ....
Where: .... Notes: ....
....
....
....

Name: .... Date: ....
Where: .... Notes: ....
....
....
....

Name: .... Date: ....
Where: .... Notes: ....
....
....
....

Name: .... Date: ....
Where: .... Notes: ....
....
....
....

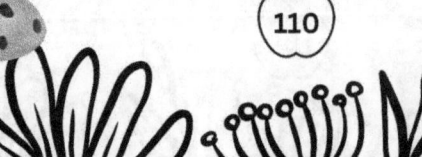

Pollinator Fan Page

Name: .... Date: ....
Where: .... Notes: ....
....
....
....

Name: .... Date: ....
Where: .... Notes: ....
....
....
....

Name: .... Date: ....
Where: .... Notes: ....
....
....
....

Actions & results:

Pollinator Fan Page

Name: .... Date: ....
Where: .... Notes: ....
....
....
....

Name: .... Date: ....
Where: .... Notes: ....
....
....
....

Name: .... Date: ....
Where: .... Notes: ....
....
....
....

Name: .... Date: ....
Where: .... Notes: ....
....
....
....

Pollinator Fan Page

Name: ……………………………………… Date: ………………………………………
Where: ……………………………………… Notes: ………………………………………
………………………………………………………………………………………………
………………………………………………………………………………………………
………………………………………………………………………………………………

Name: ……………………………………… Date: ………………………………………
Where: ……………………………………… Notes: ………………………………………
………………………………………………………………………………………………
………………………………………………………………………………………………
………………………………………………………………………………………………

Name: ……………………………………… Date: ………………………………………
Where: ……………………………………… Notes: ………………………………………
………………………………………………………………………………………………
………………………………………………………………………………………………
………………………………………………………………………………………………

Actions & results:

Harvest Tracking Sheet

Tree / Plant name	Harvest		Harvest		Harvest		Harvest		Harvest		Total weight	Grocery store price	Total cost savings
	Date	Amount harvested	Date	Amount harvested	Date	Amount harvested	Date	Amount harvested	Date	Amount harvested			

Harvest Tracking Sheet

Tree / Plant name	Harvest		Harvest		Harvest		Harvest		Harvest		Total weight	Grocery store price	Total cost savings
	Date	Amount harvested	Date	Amount harvested	Date	Amount harvested	Date	Amount harvested	Date	Amount harvested			

Harvest Tracking Sheet

Tree / Plant name	Harvest		Harvest		Harvest		Harvest		Harvest		Harvest		Total weight	Grocery store price	Total cost savings
	Date	Amount harvested	Date	Amount harvested	Date	Amount harvested	Date	Amount harvested	Date	Amount harvested	Date	Amount harvested			

Ready for some more inspiration?

Check out Sophie's books to keep your garden thriving all year round. Create your own sustainable permaculture garden, or dive deep into container gardening with proven DIY methods for composting, companion planting, seed saving, water management and pest control!
Learn how to grow your own food in harmony with nature.

Success is guaranteed!

Just scan this QR code with your phone, or use the https://Series.SophieMckay.com link to land directly on the book's Amazon page,

or
visit the Author's bookstore at
www.smartmindpublishing.com

Notes

Notes

Notes

Notes

Notes

Notes

Notes

Notes

Notes

Notes

Notes

Dot Grid Planner

Dot Grid Planner

Dot Grid Planner

Dot Grid Planner

Dot Grid Planner

Dot Grid Planner

Thanks for Reading; please leave a review!

I would be incredibly happy if you could rate my book or leave a review on Amazon.

Just scan this QR code with your phone, or visit the http://fruittreejournal.sophiemckay.com link to land directly on the book's Amazon review page.

Your review not only helps me create better books but also helps more fellow gardeners experience success in the garden and put healthy food on their family's table.

Thank you!

Sophie

Need more pages to track your garden's progress?

I've got good news for you!

Visit my website,
https://sophiemckay.com/free-resources/
to access and download free, printable pages.

These extra pages follow the same format as the book, ensuring **you can continue documenting your gardening journey with ease and familiarity**.

Whether you need more space for your planting timelines, pest control notes, or your latest garden layout ideas, these additional pages are ready to help you. **Expand your journal as your garden grows** because your green thumb adventure deserves unlimited space.

Happy gardening!

Sophie

www.ingramcontent.com/pod-product-compliance
Lightning Source LLC
Chambersburg PA
CBHW080636130526
44591CB00047B/2676